HENNA DESIGNING TUTORIAL PART-1

BASIC TO EXPERT

SUMAIYYA B JAGIRDAR

Copyright © Sumaiyya B Jagirdar
All Rights Reserved.

ISBN 978-1-63940-741-5

This book has been published with all efforts taken to make the material error-free after the consent of the author. However, the author and the publisher do not assume and hereby disclaim any liability to any party for any loss, damage, or disruption caused by errors or omissions, whether such errors or omissions result from negligence, accident, or any other cause.

While every effort has been made to avoid any mistake or omission, this publication is being sold on the condition and understanding that neither the author nor the publishers or printers would be liable in any manner to any person by reason of any mistake or omission in this publication or for any action taken or omitted to be taken or advice rendered or accepted on the basis of this work. For any defect in printing or binding the publishers will be liable only to replace the defective copy by another copy of this work then available.

Every time you buy a book and see an author dedicating the book to a person in their life, I would like to dedicate this book to a person who is reading this book.

Contents

Foreword	*vii*
Preface	*ix*
Acknowledgements	*xi*
Prologue	*xiii*
1. About Henna	1
2. Dots	6
3. Line	9
4. Circles	12
5. Humps	14
6. Swirls	16
7. Curves	18
8. Flower Petals	20
9. Fillings And Patterns	25
10. Borders	27
11. Leaf	29
12. Shapes	32
13. Drops	34
14. Basic Designs	36
Key Points & Summary	43

Foreword

This book is designed keeping in a mind a non-designer to become a professional expert henna designer on completing this book. All basic concepts from scratch are included in this book with examples to train a learner to become an expert at henna designing.

To become an expert in any aspect one must have complete knowledge of the concept that you are learning, this book includes henna designing tutorial all concepts in detail from beginning to end.

Preface

Designs in this book are drawn and explained by me, I being a Henna designer since last 15 years I have applied henna to many people for weddings and functions, all together carrying my complete experience of henna profession I have wrote this book.

Design I have included are very useful and good for learner, I have designed this book gathering my whole experience of teaching henna tutorial to my students who are now become expert professionals and earning good money out of their talent.

Acknowledgements

I want to thank them all who supported me writing this book and thank you for chosing this book for learning henna tutorial and congratulate you that you are going to be a professional henna designer on completing this tutorial book.

Prologue

Since long i was planning to write a book on henna designing course, I started many times but ended up leaving it incomplete for some reasons, bu this time by taking an inspiration from my husband i decided to write and compete this book.

My husband is my inspiration for me beginning the journey writing, I am a graphic designer and henna designing is my talent that I am blessed with from my almighty, My husband always supported me to explore my talent and achieve whatever I spired for.

CHAPTER ONE

About Henna

Mehndi (Henna) is a flowering plant and the sole species of the genus Lawsonia. It is the source of the dye henna used to dye skin, hair and fingernails, and fabrics, including silk, wool, and leather.

Henna Plant

Mehendi leaves are dried and ground to a fine powder and a smooth paste is prepared which can be packed in cones and applied on hands to get beautiful mehendi stains on hands, feet, and other body parts like the neck, back head etc.

Henna powder

A smooth paste is prepared with a proper consistency that is easy to apply on hands, the paste is poured in a cone prepared with plastic sheet and tape, the henna filled cone is tightly taped in a way that henna paste flows smoothly while applying also it doesn't overflow from the opposite side when the cone is pressed.

Henna cone

These henna cones can be stored for a long time, it is very easy and convenient for applying henna designs using cones, in the olden days people used small sticks the size of toothpick sticks to apply henna on hands, feet, and other body parts as temporary tattoos.

Henna is very famous and liked by the most in India, Pakistan, Arab countries. It is a very important celebration of applying henna to the bride's hands and feet at weddings.

Mehendi is also applied on special occasions like festivals, parties etc, not only it is used for applying temporary tattoos on hands and feet but also used for dying grey hair, applying on hair does the conditioning of hair and gives a smooth texture and dyes the grey hair, its natural coolant too, for dying hair directly paste is applied on hair by hands with or without gloves, after applying the henna paste on hair it can be washed after 30 minutes.

To get deeper colour on hair, natural ingredients like tea decoction or beetroot paste is mixed, addition tea decoction gives dark brown colour and adding beetroot paste gives burgundy colour to hair. Adding egg white conditions hair.

Mehendi Design

Mehendi designing is the art of drawing and applying henna on hands, feet, fingernails and other body parts as temporary tattoos. Learning mehendi design is easy and simple, prior knowledge of drawing or designing is not necessary, one can learn designing henna from scratch and become a master in Hanna designing in just a few days.

The very first thing in designing is getting a good knowledge of shapes and basic designs. Here below we have listed the basics of henna designing, to become a good designer begin withdrawing all below shapes and designs with a pencil in a book.

Where is henna applied?

1. Hands
2. Feet
3. Fingernails
4. Necklace
5. Baldhead
6. Waist
7. Back
8. Other body parts

Let's begin with very basic concepts of designing, for any designer, it is necessary to have strong knowledge of the basic foundation of the designing concepts, the concepts you are going to learn now are the main building blocks of your designing professional career if you are looking for a bright future in henna designing it is recommended for you to understand the importance of following basic concepts, let it may be the simplest line, you got to have the good hold on drawing.

CHAPTER TWO

Dots

Though dot is very simple and easy to draw, anyone can easily draw a dot but drawing dots in a systematic way that creates the beautiful design is very important, it's just as simple as putting a dot in the end of a sentence making it full stop but in henna designing dots are used in many places.

Here are some of the examples of dots given below, practice all these designs given below in a plain white paper book with a pencil.

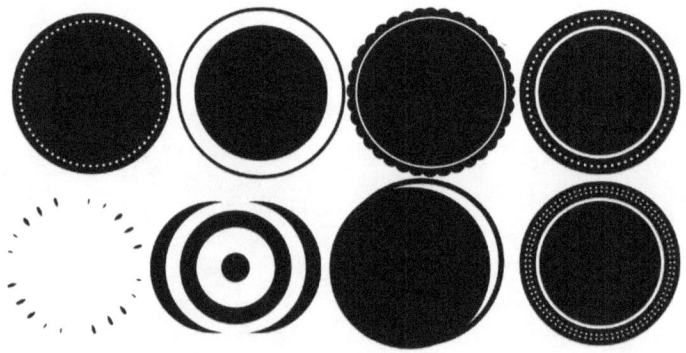

SUMAIYYA B JAGIRDAR

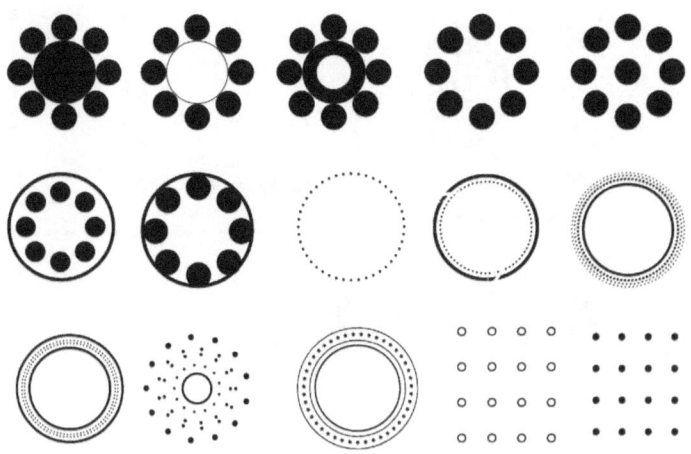

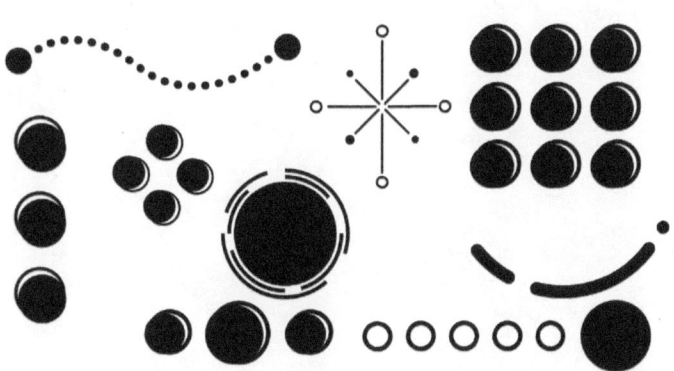

HENNA DESIGNING TUTORIAL PART-1

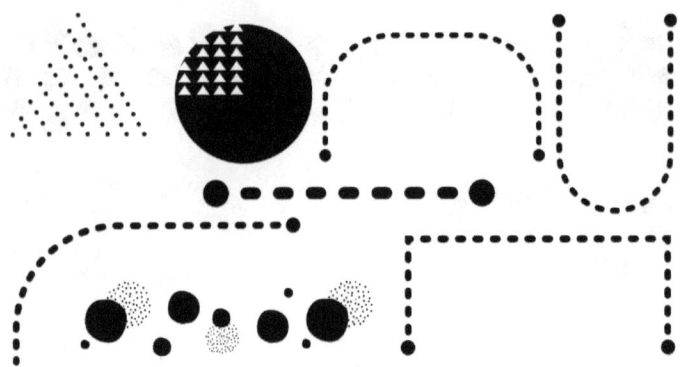

CHAPTER THREE

Line

Lines are a very basic and most important thing in designing various shapes and curves to create a beautiful design which enhances the beauty of henna on hands, though drawing lines is very simple, drawing them to create a design complementing the design applied on hands will be attractive, lines are very important in any designing, even a small single line creates a beautiful impact on design. Practising drawing these all lines will help you to be a good designer. Here are some of the examples of lines given below.

HENNA DESIGNING TUTORIAL PART-1

SUMAIYYA B JAGIRDAR

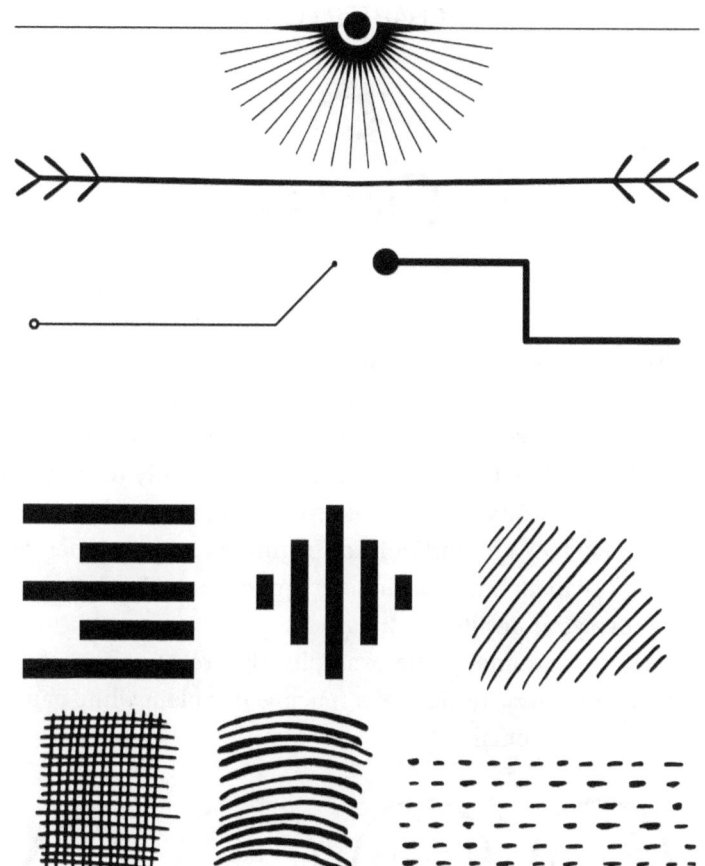

CHAPTER FOUR

Circles

Circles create beautiful henna designs. Though drawing a circle is simple yet difficult to draw it perfectly in proper shape. The alignment of Circles and double circles are used more in design, bringing perfect shapes slightly difficult as we wont be using any compass to draw perfect circle

It may feel a bit difficult for beginners to draw a perfect circle shape, but continuous practise will definitely improve your designing skills.

Here are some of the examples of circles given below, practice all these designs given below in a plain white paper book with a pencil.

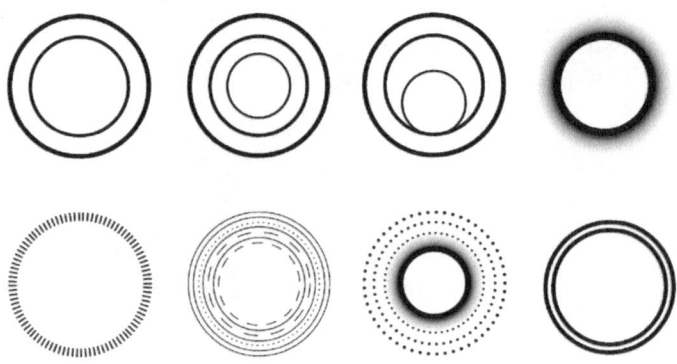

SUMAIYYA B JAGIRDAR

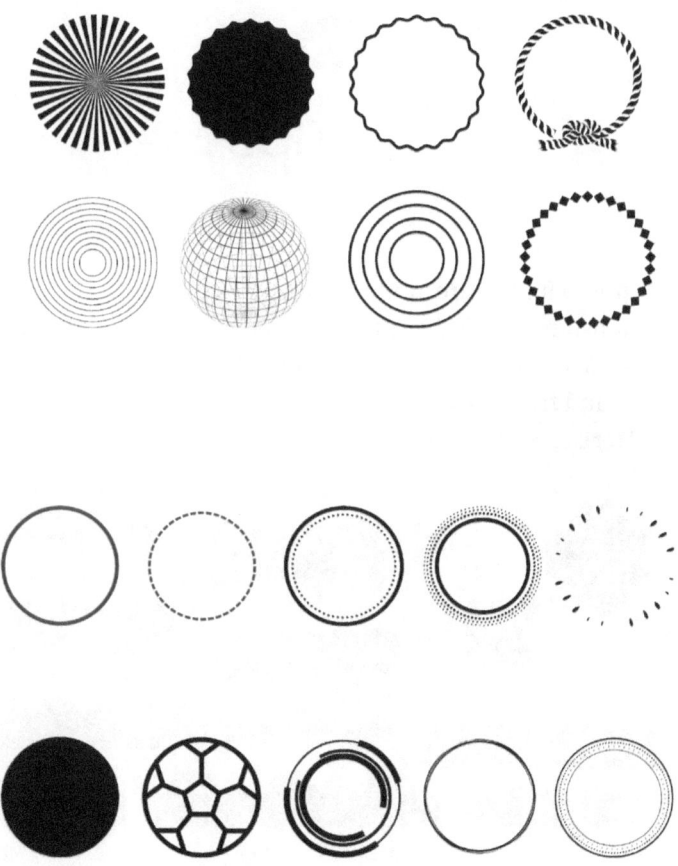

CHAPTER FIVE

Humps

Humps: Humps are dotted curve designs used on outer circumferences of shapes like circles, squares, lines etc, these give a good impact on Henna designs, drawn both in thick and thin lines

Here are some examples are given below.

SUMAIYYA B JAGIRDAR

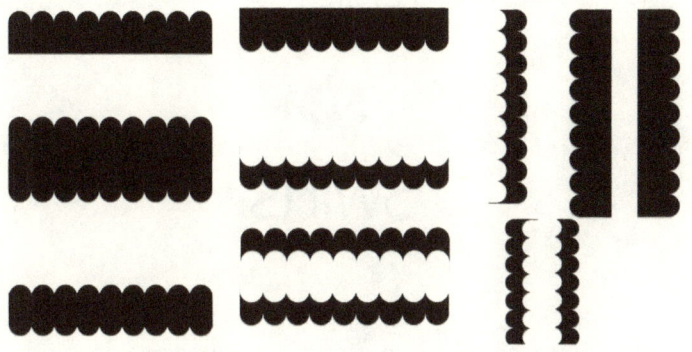

CHAPTER SIX

Swirls

Curved lines, or circles continuously drawn one on another without closing or closing its edges. A combination of Circles created swirls, curves with knots, these are like curly hair rounded, curvy lines one on the another create beautiful swirl designs.

Practice these designs in white plain sheet paper with pencil, apart from these draw the other swirl designs that you get on your mind.

A simple line with a curve becomes so beautiful when henna color comes on hands, the hands look very beautiful when henna that applied leaves stains.

CHAPTER SEVEN

Curves

Lines slightly bent are curved lines, curved lines are most easy to draw, curves are itself most beautiful lines and these lines are used to create beautiful designs, just drawing curvy lines on hands in a systematic way will create a good design. No perfect shape or size is necessary for drawing the curve lines, these can be drawn easily with freehand drawing, practicing curve lines will definitely help you good at drawing lines, drawing curvy lines is much easier than drawing straight lines, you can draw these lines in direction and add humps, swirls, circles etc. Here are some examples are given below

CHAPTER EIGHT

Flower Petals

various flower petals and shapes are the most famous designing tools in henna designing, a simple flower applied on hand is the most attractive henna design, flower designs are very favourable and are beautiful, flowers make the henna design more beautiful and elegant, petals are an important aspect of designing, you can create a variety of designs using petals.

floral designs are a must in henna, you might see many designs applied almost all are covered with floral designs, floral designs are beautiful and easy to apply and they give a very rich look on hands and other body parts.

Here are some examples are given below.

HENNA DESIGNING TUTORIAL PART-1

HENNA DESIGNING TUTORIAL PART-1

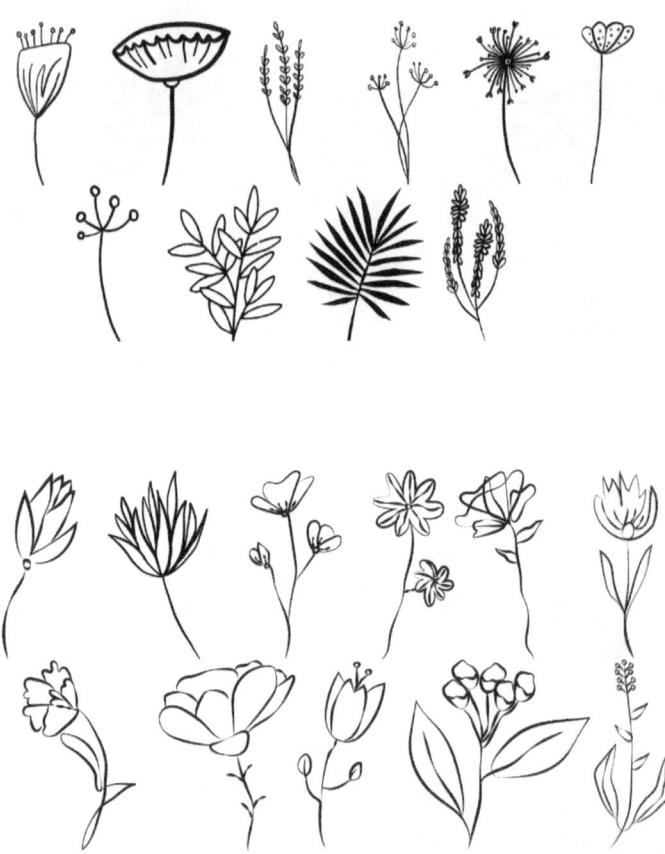

CHAPTER NINE

Fillings and patterns

The shapes in designing are filled with various designs and patterns to make them complete. filling shapes enhances the beauty, usually, shapes are filled with patterns, lines, designs etc. Simple shapes don't give that appealing look so the fillings enhance the beauty of henna designing.

Here are some examples are given below.

HENNA DESIGNING TUTORIAL PART-1

CHAPTER TEN

Borders

Borders are usually applied at the beginning or end of the design, the border can be simple two lines or design with a combination of flowers, lines, etc., border gives a beautiful look on your hands.

Here are some examples are given below.

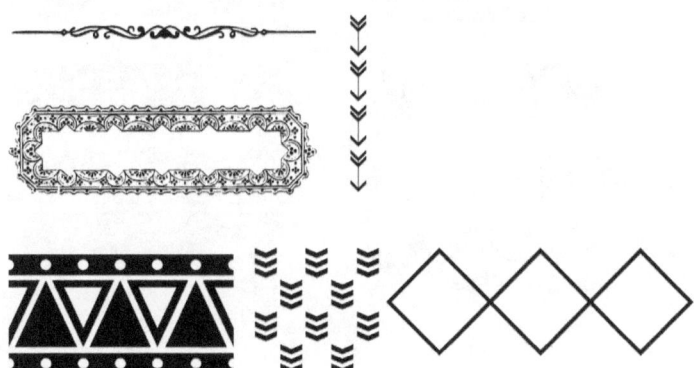

HENNA DESIGNING TUTORIAL PART-1

CHAPTER ELEVEN

Leaf

The flower looks more beautiful with its leaf beside, henna designs are also applied using flower leaves, and a variety of designs of leaves itself makes complete design.

Here are some examples are given below.

HENNA DESIGNING TUTORIAL PART-1

CHAPTER TWELVE

Shapes

shapes are a very and very important aspect of any design, not just henna designs. If you know shapes well you can design beautifully, though there are many shapes, all geometric shapes can be used in designing, shapes are very important and can be easily drawn.

Here are some examples are given below.

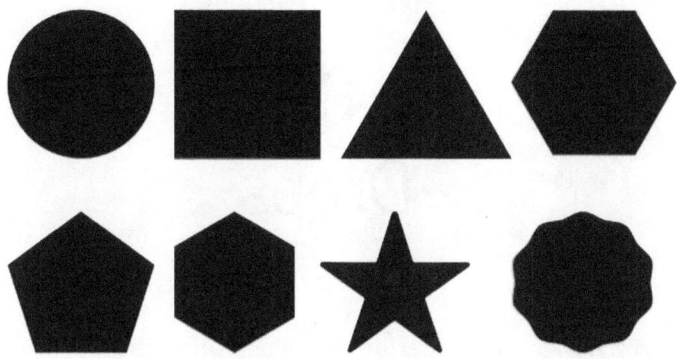

Practise above given shapes and try drawing shapes other than given in book, drawing shape improves drawing techniques, we will not be using only these shapes in henna designing, you can reshape them with your own creative ideas, creativity increases only when you try to do something that you are not knowing preiorly

CHAPTER THIRTEEN

Drops

Drop designs are water droplet like shapes, these are good supportive designs that compliment henna designing.
   Here are some examples are given below.

SUMAIYYA B JAGIRDAR

CHAPTER FOURTEEN

Basic Designs

The shapes, designs, fillings, borders etc are the basic building blocks of henna designing, to become a good designer one must know all these basic things of designing, a good practice leads to a good hold on designing.

Begin with very basic chunks and practice until you become good at drawing, once you get a good hold on drawing these it will become easy for you to apply henna design, though drawing from a pen or pencil and applying henna are completely different but it makes you familiar with shapes and designs after practising with a pencil in a book.

Here is a good collection of designs for you to learn designing henna, practice all the following designs in a plain sheet book with a pencil first, once you get a good hold on drawing designs you can move to apply henna with a cone on papers, in the beginning, you will feel difficult to hold cone, press cone to bring out henna evenly but practice will ease you on that after you get familiar with henna cone you can start applying on hands and so on.

HENNA DESIGNING TUTORIAL PART-1

HENNA DESIGNING TUTORIAL PART-1

SUMAIYYA B JAGIRDAR

HENNA DESIGNING TUTORIAL PART-1

Key Points & Summary

Key points:

First, practice all designs until you become good at these designs.

Practice using a pencil in a plain book.

Draw each design atheist twice.

Don't ignore simple designs, very basic lines and dots because they are building blocks of your design.

Continue practising daily for at least 30 minutes.

Maintain two books, one for rough designing and one for drawing perfect designs that you draw well.

Apart from the designs provided in this book try drawing from your own ideas.

Repeat the same design multiple times until you get it fine.

Summary:

We have covered all basic designs from scratch in this book. After practising all these designs you have got good designing skills now you are ready for moving on to the professional henna application. You will get all the designs, techniques and tricks of henna designing in the second part of the book.

www.ingramcontent.com/pod-product-compliance
Lightning Source LLC
LaVergne TN
LVHW041546060526
838200LV00037B/1157